Cultivating Peace and Joy

ANTHONY L. SARDELLA

authorHOUSE®

AuthorHouse™
1663 Liberty Drive
Bloomington, IN 47403
www.authorhouse.com
Phone: 1 (800) 839-8640

Published by AuthorHouse 01/04/2017

ISBN: 978-1-5246-5451-1 (sc)
ISBN: 978-1-5246-5450-4 (e)

Library of Congress Control Number: 2016920599

Print information available on the last page.

Contents

Affirmations 1

Awaken Your Inner Spirit 3

Balance 5

Be a Light for Others... 7

Breathe 9

The Bumps in the Road 11

Chasing Happiness.. 13

Clarity 15

Cultivating the Garden 17

Detachment... 19

Discomfort Is Our Best Teacher............................ 21

Exercising the Mind and Body 23

Gratitude 25

Helping Others... 27

Honesty 29

Identifying Our Triggers 31

Inherent Peace.. 33

The Journey... 35

Kindness and Compassion 37

Laugh and Smile Daily............................. 39

Letting Go of the Past 41

Life Has Different Plans for Us 43

The Little Things in Life 45

Live Today... 47

Living Your Dream 49

Lose Yourself 51

Making Friends with Our Anxieties and Fears..... 53

Making the Shift 55

Mindfulness 57

The Moment Will Take Care of Itself 59

Nature...61

No One Is Perfect.. 63

Patience.. 65

Putting Down the Backpack 67

Religion and Spirituality...................................... 69

Riding the Wave 71

Rise above the Suffering 73

Savor Today 75

Shutting the Valve 77

Stillness.. 79

Understanding Your Body 81

Unlocking the Door 83

What Comes Next 85

Ashley -

For your strength, courage, grace, and loving hugs.

Acknowledgments

I would like to thank my two sons, Michael and Anthony Sardella, for helping me put this book together. Thanks also to Carol Angerone, Geetha Chandrasekhar, Dana Ianniello, Noreen Mahony, and Nicholas and Linda Pasquarello for their editing and for bringing clarity to my ideas.

Cover Photo by Dennis Goodman

Introduction

Living in today's world has gotten tougher, and we are constantly being pulled in many different directions. By cultivating the seeds of peace and joy in our daily lives, we achieve a greater sense of well-being. Each short section and quote will help guide you through transforming a new or forgotten way of thinking. I recommend you take your time reading this book, so as not to overwhelm yourself putting these practices into place. There is a reflection part after each quote at the end of every section, so you can write down any thoughts or feelings that arise. There is no quick fix for finding more peace and joy in our lives, but with commitment, time, and patience, you will begin to see the transformation from within.

Affirmations

Affirmations are reminders to ourselves that we can do anything we set out to do. Affirming the intention we have today will give us direction and keep us on track. Whether we write them down, say them out loud, or say them to ourselves, affirmations hold us accountable for our desired action. Practicing affirmations should be on our list of things to do each day, preferably early in the day so our intentions can manifest throughout the day. Eventually, our affirmations will become reality and give us strength, courage, wisdom, and a feeling of grace.

Fill your cup daily so you will never be thirsty.

Reflection...

Awaken Your Inner Spirit

Deep inside ourselves, there is an inner spirit that moves and motivates us. It also gives us strength, courage, and guidance. At times during our lives, we tend to lose our spirit for various reasons. This innate quality that lives inside all of us can be awakened at any time by looking from within, without judgment, and seeing our true selves. Our inner spirit will guide us and help us achieve lasting peace and joy in our lives. With time and some soul-searching, we will begin to see the transformation within ourselves, just as a caterpillar turns into a beautiful butterfly.

Live life. There is no perfect place, time, or situation to live it.

Reflection...

Balance

Living a balanced life in today's world is getting harder and harder. Life is like a seesaw, with its many ups and downs. We are constantly being pulled in many different directions, and most times we drain ourselves physically and mentally. We need to reset our thinking and change our mind-set in order to live a more balanced life. Everyone has different ideas of what a balanced life is; what works for one person may not work for another. Just think about what we really need in our lives and what is most important to us. Finding balance is a journey, not a destination. By breaking an unhealthy or unbalanced cycle, we will feel more relaxed and live more in the present moment.

*Life is not black or white. There
is much gray in between.*

Reflection...

Be a Light for Others

Many people we may know are living in darkness and are having trouble finding their way. We have the opportunity to bring light into their world. Helping someone in need is one of the greatest gifts we can give: it will have a domino effect that will help countless people, including ourselves. By taking a step back and putting ourselves into others' shoes we will get a different perspective on people and how they feel. A simple gesture can go a long way. We may not even know the impact we will make but just think about the people who have opened our hearts and the change they have made in our lives. By helping others, we can move the focus from ourselves to something more meaningful, which will give us a greater sense of self.

Every snowflake does count.

Reflection...

Breathe

We usually do not notice our breath unless we're exercising, out in the cold or beginning to feel anxious. If we can take a few moments each day to focus on our breathing, we will begin to see many beneficial effects. This can be practiced either with our eyes open or closed. Slowly take a breath, let your belly expand, and then let it out slowly. Doing this for a few minutes a couple of times a day will help us feel calmer and more relaxed. Most importantly, our thoughts will disappear while doing this exercise, as long as we focus on our breathing. We will begin to feel less anxious and more peaceful.

Peace and joy are but a breath away.

Reflection...

The Bumps in the Road

Along the way in life, we will hit many bumps in the road. Some we won't even notice, while others can swallow us up whole. Life has its own plan for us, which can conflict with our own. Life cannot exist without pain and suffering; eventually they catch up to all of us. The hardest part is going through it. However, inner peace and joy are always at hand; even though we may not notice during the most difficult or trying times, they are inherent in all of us. We cannot feel them when we're hurting, but in time we will heal and become stronger people because of them. The road we are on has more clear stretches than bumps. Being mindful and living in the present moment will lessen the jolt when it does happen.

We are not alone with our thoughts and fears.

Reflection...

Chasing Happiness

We often look ahead to things that will make us happier, saying to ourselves that once this is over and done, we will feel better. We are chasing after something that's right in front of us. Happiness comes from within; recognizing it is the difficult part. Whether we're looking for our next raise or a new relationship, happiness cannot be found from outside things. We often blame others because we are unhappy. That is a sign that we are not taking responsibility for our own well-being. We have a choice to be happy or to not be happy. It's up to us to realize the choice is our own, and once we understand that, it will bring us one step closer to being happier with ourselves and others.

Stop running, and walk with mindfulness today.

Reflection...

Clarity

We often get lost in the labyrinth of life, at times not knowing which way to turn. We never see the full picture of where we are; the maze of life we're in seems infinite. We hope one day we will find the finish line. However, in life the journey is more important than the destination. When feeling lost, like you're in a maze, view yourself from above, and see how silly you look trying to make the right turn in order to find a way out. We often put ourselves in these situations; by eliminating the barriers around us, we will begin to see greater clarity in our lives and have fewer obstacles in our way.

The journey is the destination we seek.

Reflection...

Cultivating the Garden

If we want to bear the fruit of peace and joy, we need to cultivate the garden daily. The longer we wait, the more difficult it will be to restore the balance. Putting in time on a daily basis is necessary to make peace and joy central in our lives. As we picture our garden as ourselves, imagine if we do not water it, nourish the soil, pick the weeds, or care for it. Our well-being will become compromised by not taking care of ourselves. By taking out a small amount of time each day, we will be better prepared for what life has in store for us.

Spread the seeds of happiness.

Reflection...

Detachment

As we go through life, we accumulate many things and try to hold on to what we have. This holds true for things both physical and mental. Life is impermanent, although we don't treat it as such. The more we have, the more stuff there is to weigh us down. Detachment does not mean giving up our worldly possessions and being by ourselves. Letting go of the mind-set that we need to control things will lighten our load and make us feel more balanced. There is much freedom to be had when we detach ourselves from what is weighing us down. Usually, the more we try to control, the less control we have over things.

Let life play itself out without interference.

Reflection...

Discomfort Is Our Best Teacher

We often try to avoid whatever is uncomfortable because we are not used to making it an opportunity for ourselves. At that time we have the chance to be fully aware of what is going on and accept what is transpiring. We will bring about a sense of calm by letting go and acknowledging that we cannot control the situation. Embracing what is uncomfortable in life is a great teacher; we can grow from these experiences as a person, though it will not be easy. Taking the opportunity to pray, meditate, or exercise will give us a sense of well-being instead of anxiety. The ability to grow as a person in times of trouble is innate in all of us. Having a way to navigate the labyrinth of a complex life thrown at us not only benefits ourselves but others around us as well.

Forcing a solution results in disappointment.

Reflection...

Exercising the Mind and Body

We need to exercise both our mind and body daily; just think of all the health benefits there are. Whether we meditate or do something physical, the initial phase should be gradual, in order to avoid overwhelming ourselves. Everyone has his or her own way to accomplish a goal; there is no one right way. The ultimate goal is to give ourselves greater health and peace within. Doing something for both our mind and body can greatly enhance our lives. It takes commitment to continue along this path, but with time and patience, we will begin to see the benefit and transformation within ourselves. It not only benefits us but also helps how we deal with others as well.

Exercise is the gateway to a happier lifestyle.

Reflection...

Gratitude

There are so many things to be grateful for, but most times we do not recognize them. We often take things for granted and do not appreciate what is in front of us. Acknowledging what we have instead of what we don't have is the first step. Whether it's the place we live, the food we eat, the people in our lives, or the countless things we should be grateful for. Being aware of the abundance around us helps us look at those who are in real need. By picking something every day to be grateful for, we will begin to see how much we really have.

Be grateful for what you have today because it can be gone tomorrow.

Reflection...

Helping Others

The greatest joy we can experience in life is helping others. There seems to be too much attention placed on ourselves today. By accumulating things, we tend to get lost from within, which takes us away from our true selves. We are the caretakers of society and by neglecting to help others we are hurting ourselves and the people living in our community. There is great joy on both sides when people help one another. Our hearts will lighten and the barriers we built around ourselves will begin to soften. We do not need to make a grand gesture; the simple act of smiling or opening a door for someone will foster loving kindness. Kindness is contagious; spread it with love and happiness.

We are helping ourselves when we help others.

Reflection...

Honesty

We cannot find peace and joy in our lives if we are not honest with ourselves and others around us. Honesty creates a sense of well-being from within, while deception carries the opposite effect. It is easier to lie than to be truthful, which is why some of us take that path. Having an honest heart will give us grace we need to carry us through the most difficult times. We will not feel weighed down by the burden of dishonesty, as long as we live a life of truth—for ourselves as well as others. Honesty is the foundation on which we can live a gentle, purposeful life.

*Living a virtuous life will give us
all the freedom we seek.*

Reflection...

Identifying Our Triggers

We all have trigger points that lead us away from what we're seeking. Identifying such triggers is extremely important so that we can acknowledge what is uncomfortable. Then we can develop a strategy to help us navigate through these emotions; in time we will be able to work through any situation that is put in front of us. When something annoys us, it is a great opportunity to practice the techniques we have developed along the way. Making peace with what ails us is a necessary step to finding our true selves.

*We can stop searching when we realize
we don't have all the answers.*

Reflection...

Inherent Peace

Peace is inherent in all of us. Everyone has the ability to tap into his or her inner self, to feel a sense of grace that lightens the mind and body. It's almost impossible to feel peaceful all the time, especially in the world we live in today. Our thoughts will stray because we are human, and we will encounter challenging times throughout our lifetime. At these moments we need to remember that peace is only a breath away and that it is always with us. We need to find ways to constantly remind ourselves because we can easily forget. As we continue this practice, we will start to see a transformation within ourselves. This change will awaken the true, peaceful self that is inherent in all of us. Our spiritual sense of being will create better balance and tranquility in our lives.

The uncluttered mind is a still one.

Reflection...

The Journey

Life is a journey, yet many of us treat it as a destination we need to get to. It's up to us to live a life filled with love, compassion, and purpose. We only get one chance at living, and we will make many mistakes along the way that we can learn from. Our journey will be filled with many surprises, both good and bad. By embracing the now, we will no longer need to look at life as a destination that continually changes. Life is good if we allow it to be. There is nothing permanent about the path we are taking. Living in the present moment will keep us grounded and connected. Helping others and staying positive is essential for living a full and balanced life.

Life is a balancing act. Just when we think we've figured things out, life has other plans for us.

Reflection...

Kindness and Compassion

In order to cultivate peace and joy in our lives, kindness and compassion must be present. Both of these qualities are inherent in all of us. Being gentle, courteous, and pleasant is the foundation from which kindness comes. We, as individuals, need to have kindness ourselves as well as for others around us. Having empathy for other people's suffering is the basis for compassion. Understanding the suffering of others and helping them out in times of need shows a sense of humanity and benevolence to society. Kindness and compassion are present in all of us.

Enjoy the ride; there's only one turn for each of us.

Reflection...

Laugh and Smile Daily

Many of us take ourselves too seriously. We often miss out on things in life we should be enjoying. We need a break from the daily struggles, laughing at something funny or at ourselves is a good way to lead a happier life. We don't need to go to a comedy show to laugh; life gives us the material on a daily basis. Laughing is also contagious. There are many positive effects we can get out of laughter, which helps both the body and the mind. Smiling is also a great mood-changer for ourselves and others around us.

*Give yourself a smile each morning
when you wake up.
It's a great way to start your day.*

Reflection...

Letting Go of the Past

We often beat ourselves up over the past and how we could have done things differently. Unfortunately, we cannot bring back the past to make changes to what we have already done. Replaying the past in our minds is counterproductive; there is nothing we can do but learn from our experiences. We do not live in a perfect world, nor could a person make all the right choices in life. We're not infallible; we are human. Most of us learn from our mistakes, which make us the people we are today. Whether it's something we did, didn't do, or had done to us, letting go of the past is essential to our well-being. By looking back, we can never be fully in the present.

*Living with regrets is like swimming
with a fifty-pound weight.*

Reflection...

Life Has Different Plans for Us

When we start to grow up, we picture how we want life to be. There are no roadblocks in how we envision our future; there are only goals and dreams we aspire to. As we live our lives, we come across obstacles that are placed in our way. These obstacles take us further away from how we want to live. As life changes, we try to cling to the life we long for. Life has different plans for us than we have for ourselves. Life has many new doors that will open for us, if we allow them to. The future we planned may not turn out the way we wanted it to, but we need to live the life that is put in front of us. We cannot predict the future or change the past but we can live in the present with happiness and gratitude for what we have.

*Surrender to the present because we can't
control the future or change the past.*

Reflection...

The Little Things in Life

The little things in life outweigh the material things we try to accumulate, whether it's a bigger house, a new iPhone, or a seventy-inch TV. However there are some things money can't buy. One of those things is happiness. We often pass up and don't appreciate the simple things in our lives that are free—watching the sunset, the smell of a flower, the laughter of a child, or a dinner with loved ones. Taking the time to acknowledge the beauty of what life has to offer will give us a greater feeling of well-being. Sharing these moments with others will greatly enhance the relationships we have. Remembering the little things will slow us down and give us more clarity.

Joy is what we make of it.

Reflection...

Live Today

We have a daily opportunity to put forth an intention that we would like to practice. Adding a word or phrase after "live today..." will give us the opportunity to reset our thinking. During the day, if we find we're losing patience, we can then say "live today with patience." This daily practice will guide us to live in the present and accept how we feel without judgment or fear. We can live today... with peace and joy, without worry, with happiness, etc. It's up to us how we fill in the blank. By doing this exercise on a regular basis, we will begin to see the transformation from within.

Live today.

Reflection...

Living Your Dream

Many of us wait for tomorrow while we're missing today. We often envision how we want our lives to be, yet we do nothing about it. Why not live the way we dream? For many, there is something that is holding us back, whether it's fear, failure, etc. Sometimes we just have to jump in and experience what life has to offer. Life is good, and we only get one chance at it. So why not live the best life we can? Otherwise, as time goes by, we may regret not having lived the life we always dreamed of.

Life does not give us days back,
so make every day count.

Reflection...

Lose Yourself

By staying in the same presence of mind that we are typically in, we are destined to remain in the status quo, without being aware of the present moment. By losing ourselves, the potential for fully being aware is at hand. Letting go and breaking our old way of thinking is necessary to accomplish this task. Stepping out of our comfort zone will push us to different levels of understanding, which will enable us to live a more balanced and meaningful life. We cannot hold on to life's ever-changing movement, so we need to lose ourselves in order to find what we are looking for.

*By casting away our fears, we will
then reel in our true self.*

Reflection...

Making Friends with Our Anxieties and Fears

Anxieties and fears do not need to overtake the mind and body. We first have to recognize what they are and why they are present. Once this is accomplished, we can then make friends with our anxieties and fears. Meditation is a good way to alleviate these troubles. While meditating, we should name and acknowledge what is bothering us. Many thoughts and emotions may pop up, but we should look at them without judgment and let them dissipate in our minds. As we breathe in, we can inhale inherent peace and exhale our anxieties and fears.

*Fears and anxieties are
opportunities, not obstacles.*

Reflection...

Making the Shift

Life goes on, whether we like it or not. Most times we're not ready for what is in store for us. Change is hard for many people, but we have to make the shift; if we don't we may get stuck. Not knowing what lies ahead of us can be a scary and liberating experience. We cannot hold on to things forever; life is impermanent. Surrendering to the uncertainty that exists in life will lead us to acceptance and peacefulness from within. Not moving with the changing times will inhibit how we live our life. It takes strength and courage to keep on moving with the changes that are in front of us.

*You can choose a path, or one
will be laid out for you.*

Reflection...

Mindfulness

Being mindful can lead us to greater peace and joy in our lives. We can achieve this by just living in the present and accepting what is happening to us at that given moment. We often let our minds run away, which leads to greater stress. By staying in the moment, we cannot let the past or future interfere with our present. Daily practice of mindfulness is needed in order to calm the racing mind. Acknowledging the feelings and emotions that are happening to us in the present and not judging them are what mindfulness is all about.

*We create our own drama when we're
not living in the present moment.*

Reflection...

The Moment Will Take Care of Itself

As humans, we worry about things we can't control. Our minds race and our hearts pound with fear. We are not God and cannot control all aspects of life, yet we feel the need to do this anyway. The moment will take care of itself, whether we worry or not. By freeing ourselves from the notion that we are in control of life, we accept the fact that life is impermanent and we cannot hold on to things. Imagine how well we could feel if we didn't put our minds and bodies through the daily stress of worrying. Remember, when we begin to worry, the moment will take care of itself.

Perfection only exists in our minds.

Reflection...

Nature

There is beauty all around us, we just have to stop and take it in. Whether we're hiking in the mountains or walking along the beach, we can learn so much from nature. It will calm and relax us both mentally and physically. A delicate balance exists between people and the environment we live in. Nature provides us with everything we need to live. It's most important that we treat our environment with the greatest amount of reverence. Nature will nourish us in many ways; step into it and be fed. Peace is innate in all of us; nature is the bridge to get there.

Embrace uncertainty; it is your best teacher.

Reflection...

No One Is Perfect

We all know no one is perfect, even though some people may act that way at times. We will make many mistakes over a lifetime; that's what makes us human. There is plenty of opportunity to learn from our mistakes if we are open to it. Many of us put pressure on ourselves to be infallible. We are just like everyone else, a person who has to come to terms with his or her own fallibility. We will realize that we not only need to forgive ourselves but others as well. This will then lighten our hearts and free our minds of the idea of being perfect.

There are many steps in life.
Take them one at a time.

Reflection...

Patience

There are times in life when we need to practice patience. Most times there is nothing we can do to change the situation we're in. Whether stuck in traffic or waiting for a phone call, we can become anxious when things don't go our way. We cannot affect the future or the outcome of things that are not in our control. Allowing our hearts to accept things as they are will soften the mind and body. We can use the situation we are in as an opportunity to grow spiritually. By practicing patience, we not only help ourselves, but can help others around us as well by having the ability to stay peaceful.

Slow down for life otherwise it will pass you by.

Reflection...

Putting Down the Backpack

There are many things in life that weigh us down, and we continue to pack them on. The mind and body can only take a certain amount of stress before it starts to break down. We often get caught up in life's events and neglect to take notice of what is actually weighing us down. As we get pulled in so many directions, it becomes almost impossible to have a balanced life. The first step toward balance is to put down the backpack of things that is weighing us down. Only when we take the load off our shoulders, can we fully understand how life was really weighing us down. We have to remember that the backpack will continually go back on if we do not remain aware of it. It may take a thousand times to practice taking it off, but each time we take it off, it will give us a sense of acknowledgment and peace. Eventually, we will notice that our worries will become lighter and we will become more relaxed with ourselves. This process does not happen overnight, it takes time to unload everything we have been carrying with us.

We cannot hold on to the things we lose.

Reflection...

Religion and Spirituality

There are two very important components in living a balanced life: religion and spirituality. Some people may be more religious than spiritual or vice versa, while others may have a strong foundation in both. In many cases, these two components overlap one another. Taking care of our well-being for our spirit and soul will give us greater clarity and peacefulness in our daily life. Believing in a greater power will give life greater meaning and purpose. Setting time out every day to pray, meditate, or reflect is necessary if we want to live life in the present moment. There are endless positive benefits we can receive from religion and spirituality.

Our Creator has given us the seeds of peace and joy; it's up to us to cultivate them.

Reflection...

Riding the Wave

Waves are continuous, they ebb and flow, there is no stopping them. As we live, we feel we're riding on a wave that is different from the ones before. Each wave has its own characteristics, most times we have no choice but to ride out the wave, often filled with fear and anxiety. The more fearful we are, the worse the ride is going to be. Life is fluid, with constant change; we cannot control the wave or life itself. Sometimes we just have to go along for the ride, not knowing where the wave is going to break. If we fall, all we can do is hold our breath, come to the surface, and realize the ride was not as scary as we once thought it would be.

Don't let life pass you by.

Reflection...

Rise above the Suffering

Suffering is inevitable; there is no way around it. We suffer from different afflictions, whether physical or emotional. It affects our mind and body when we suffer. It's easy to get lost in a spiral descent, seeing no light in the darkness. At this point we need to find a way to rise above the suffering. It is inherent in all of us to be able to do so. It may take time, and we may stumble along the way, but there is always a way to rise above. Even if we have a problem doing this for ourselves, we still need to do it for the people around us. In doing so, we will find courage to rise above our own suffering. Taking the focus off ourselves will enable us to lighten the mind and body. We are stronger than we think we are.

Face your fears while walking with your Creator.

Reflection...

Savor Today

Savor today - yesterday has passed, and tomorrow is in the future. Think about how we savor each bite of our favorite meal. Why can't today be like that? It can, if we live in the present moment each day. Just imagine if there was no tomorrow, how much we would savor every moment by not worrying about what tomorrow will bring. Making the most of each day will bring great benefits to our physical and mental well-being. It will bring greater peace and joy within our lives, and we will be able to appreciate what life has to offer us.

Love life today.

Reflection...

Shutting the Valve

The racing mind is very difficult to catch up to, yet we continue to try. The overflowing of our thoughts weighs us down considerably. Finding and holding on to the space in between our thoughts is quite challenging. By being in the present moment, our racing mind will subside. When our thoughts begin to overrun us, just consider the mind like a valve; we can open it when it's needed and close it when we get overwhelmed. Somewhere in the middle is a happy medium. Having the ability to open and close the thoughts that go through our minds is a powerful tool we have. There is not a specific way to do this; everyone has to figure out what works for them. Slowing down our thoughts can bring a healthier mind and body.

*Leave your worries behind or put
them off to another day.*

Reflection...

Stillness

Life keeps us going at a rapid pace, rushing from one thing to the next. There never seems to be enough time in the day to get everything done. We need to set some time aside for ourselves, to stop the moving and constant chatter that runs through our minds. We need to still the mind and body on a regular basis in order to achieve greater balance in our lives. By doing so, we will feel more relaxed and calm. We often find excuses that we don't have the time to be still. Life gives us opportunities to take advantage of being still, we just have to recognize them. Tranquility will become more prevalent in our minds and bodies if we take the time to be still. Unplugging ourselves will lighten our load so we don't burn ourselves out. It takes daily practice to still our minds and bodies.

We all start out as a caterpillar and cannot turn into a butterfly until it's time.

Reflection...

Understanding Your Body

Our body plays a vital role in our physical and mental health. No two bodies are the same, it's very important for us to understand the balance that works best for us, whether it be the food we eat, the exercises we do, or the way we approach our mental health. It is an ongoing process because we are constantly changing as we get older, as are the different situations that life offers us. Sometimes we cannot figure out the balance ourselves. That's why we look to books, friends, and professionals to help us find our best self. There are no quick fixes to this process. Most often it is trial and error to figure out what works best for us. Perseverance is needed to achieve our goal.

If you cannot find the answers, seek guidance.

Reflection...

Unlocking the Door

We often find ourselves trapped behind the doors we unknowingly locked. The reason why we have locked them really doesn't matter; what matters most is unlocking these doors and walking through them. Walking through these doors in and of itself represents a new beginning—to embrace life and what it has to offer. We would have never known what lies ahead of us if we never had the courage to unlock the door and walk through. We all have the key within ourselves. Although some of us misplace or even lose the key, it is still inherent in all of us.

Believe in yourself; the possibilities are endless.

Reflection...

What Comes Next

Many of us are looking ahead and not paying attention to the present. Life will take care of itself, whether we like it or not. Trying to find answers to the unknown is quite impossible; there are so many variables that are unknown. Letting life play itself out will give us more time to live in the moment and not stress about controlling life's unknowns. Although there are times in our lives we have to plan for, we need to adjust to life's uncertainty. It can be exciting not to have our lives fully planned out. It gives us the opportunity to go along with life's natural changes and enjoy what lies in front of us.

Live today without worry.

Reflection...

Printed in the United States
By Bookmasters